STATISTICAL POWER TRIP

How the Analysis of Statistical Power will Help you Win Grants, Get Published, and have a Successful Research Career!

PAUL D. ELLIS

Statistical Power Trip:
How the Analysis of Statistical Power will help you Win Grants, Get Published, and Have a Successful Research Career!

ISBN: 978-1-927230-57-2

Published by MadMethods, an imprint of KingsPress.org,
PO Box 66145, Beach Haven, Auckland 0749, New Zealand.

To get this title in other formats and to find other titles in the MadMethods series, visit www.MadMethods.co

Version: 1.2 (September 2020)

Dedication: For my teachers.

What readers are saying about
The Essential Guide to Effect Sizes

Who knew statistics was this interesting?

— Amazon Reviewer

Exceptionally lucid overview of power analysis, effect sizes, and sample size calculations. Wonderful book.

— Stijn Debrouwere

I work with very smart people who design studies but don't typically have rigorous mathematical training. When someone wants to learn about how sample size justifications and power calculations work, this is the first book that I recommend. It is exceptionally well written. It explains the key ideas that underlay power and sample size calculations without getting bogged down in mathematical rigor. If you are not a statistician and you want to learn about sample size estimation or how to think about how to quantify meaningful differences this is the book you want.

— Amazon Reviewer

This stats reform business is serious, we all need to get into it, and Paul's book is a terrific guide. Enjoy!

— Geoff Cumming

I thoroughly enjoyed this and read it twice. Later I incorporated it into a module in my advanced stats class for doctoral students. The topic was perfect for them, and the comfortable writing style made the book a delight to read. As noted by the author– some people write to impress and others to instruct. This book is for instruction.

— Wm. A. Sands

An excellent primer.

— Hendrick McDonald

I've recommended this book to other grad students in my classes. It's a short read with a ton of good stuff in it. It doesn't try to teach you everything about statistics, but it does a good job of teaching you how to think responsibly with statistics.

— Amazon Reviewer

"When I stumbled on power analysis… it was as if I had died and gone to heaven."

— Jacob Cohen (1990: 1308)

Contents

Why do I need this book?

Some researchers analyze words, others analyze numbers. This book is for the number-crunchers. Specifically, it is for anyone who relies on statistical inference to draw conclusions about real world effects.

But don't panic—this is not a statistics book, at least not in the usual sense. In this book you won't learn how to run a *t* test or do a logit regression or any of that stuff. What you will learn is how to ensure that whatever test you run has sufficient power to do what it is supposed to do.

Five reasons to read this book

There are at least five compelling reasons why researchers should be concerned about the statistical power of their studies:

1. Running a power analysis prevents you from engaging in research that is destined to fail. Many of the effects we study are small, yet surveys regularly show that most studies lack the power to

detect such effects. Insufficient statistical power leads to multiple problems such as wasted resources and the misdirection of future research. This book will teach you how to run a simple power analysis that will protect you from engaging in studies that are fatally under-powered or wastefully over-powered.

2. Running a power analysis improves your funding prospects. Cognizant of the dangers of insufficient power, funding agencies are increasingly asking researchers to submit the results of power analyses along with their research proposals. They want to know, "Does the proposed study have the power needed to detect the effect of interest?" Researchers who comply with these requests are setting themselves up for success, both in terms of attracting research funding and doing meaningful research.

3. Running a power analysis improves your publication prospects. Following recommendations made by the APA, editors and journal reviewers are increasingly asking authors to report on the statistical power of their studies. They want to see evidence that the study had sufficient power to detect effects of interest. Authors who provide

such evidence (e.g., the results of a power analysis) are more likely to have their papers published than those who don't.

4. Learning about statistical power will liberate you from potentially damaging allegiance to the $p < .05$ standard of statistical significance by getting you to articulate your expectations regarding the relative threat of Type I and Type II errors. It will also prompt you to evaluate results in terms of the evidence and protect you from assigning substantive significance to results that are merely statistically significant.

5. Learning about statistical power will help you avoid Type II errors. In a culture that is obsessed with the minimization of Type I errors, Type II errors have become endemic. This book will show you five ways to minimize the threat of these errors.

As we will see, the analysis of statistical power is neither difficult nor time-consuming, yet the payoffs are considerable.

A good power analysis offers enormous bang for your buck.

Who wrote this book?

I began my research career as a qualitative researcher (think case studies), but I soon succumbed to the dark side and became a number-cruncher. I have conducted countless studies in several countries using a variety of methods and statistical programs. I have won awards for research and been successful in winning numerous research grants. I have had numerous papers published in top tier journals and served on several editorial review boards.

You might consider me a successful researcher, but the truth is more complicated. I haven't told you about my many failures—projects that went nowhere, data that revealed nothing, and analyses that were flat-out wrong. One thing that long troubled me was the question that hung over every new project. *Would this study bear fruit?* Despite the toolbox of skills that I had acquired, I was never 100 percent certain that my research investments would pay off, and this bothered me.

Do you know what it's like to spend three to four years on a project only to find nothing particularly interesting? Have you ever had to bin a project because there was nothing there? Or maybe there was—you could feel it—but you couldn't see it. The results didn't quite pan out.

These are tough realities for the best of us, but for Ph.D. students betting their latent careers on a single project, they are terrifying. I have seen more than one Ph.D. project come crashing down because data carefully collected and analyzed revealed little of interest.

For a long time I thought this uncertainty was a normal part of the research process. I even tried to convince myself that there was something exciting about not knowing whether a study would bear fruit. But, in truth, there is nothing exciting about wasting years of work. It's frustrating in the extreme.

Then I stumbled upon meta-analysis and the all-important concept of effect size. That, in turn, led me to the analysis of statistical power.

It was like somebody had switched on all the lights.

I began to understand that much of the uncertainty I had lived with was nothing more than ignorance on my part. Like an investor buying shares in the Titanic, I was setting myself up to fail.

I was both thrilled to discover power analysis and saddened that I hadn't learned this stuff sooner. None of my methods teachers and none of the methods books on my shelf said anything about it. The few texts that did mention it struck me as unnecessarily dense and hard to read.

Rather than curse the darkness I decided to light a candle, so I wrote my own book; *The Essential Guide to Effect Sizes: Statistical Power, Meta-Analysis, and the Interpretation of Research Results*. It's a comprehensive yet jargon-free introduction to the largely ignored subject of effect sizes and their role in meta- and statistical power analysis.

When my book came out I set up a promotional website called www.effectsizefaq.com. The site has helpful tips and tricks along with links to useful resources such as online calculators. The site has proven quite popular attracting millions of page views.

By monitoring traffic on the site, I have discovered that researchers and students are looking for straight-forward answers to three important questions:

(1) What is an effect size?
(2) How do I calculate the statistical power of my study?
(3) How do I draw definitive conclusions from inconclusive studies?

The book you are reading answers the second question. Two other books in the MadMethods series, *Effect Size Matters* and *Meta-Analysis Made Easy,* answer the first and third questions respectively. If you are unfamiliar with the concept of effect sizes, I recommend reading the first one before diving into this one. A good understanding of effect sizes and how to measure them is an essential precursor to power analysis. And if you wish to learn how to harvest effect sizes from past research, the third book provides a step-by-step guide. (Value tip: You get three-books-in-one for a low price in the omnibus version.)

Why did I write these books when I have already written a perfectly good text? Because students are poor and researchers are busy. You probably don't have six months to come to grips with these new subjects. You just want the short version.

Voila!

This book is designed to be a quick and easy introduction to the analysis of statistical power. By the time you're done, you should be able to run power analyses and design studies with sufficient power to detect the effects you are seeking. You will be attuned to the very real threat of Type II errors, and you will be equipped to deal with this risk.

Paul D. Ellis

What is statistical power? And how can I get some?

Let's begin with a plain-English definition:

> Statistical power describes the probability that a statistical test will correctly identify a genuine effect.

By genuine effect I mean an effect that is real as opposed to imaginary. For instance, if smoking has an effect on lung cancer, a properly empowered test should be able to detect this effect. If smoking has no effect lung cancer, then all the statistical power in the world won't help you prove that it does.

Statistical power will not help you see things that aren't there but it will help you see things that are. Like the magnification power in binoculars, the more statistical power you have, the easier it is to see things.

As long as the effect you are looking for is genuine—meaning, it exists in the real world—a study with sufficient statistical power will have a good chance of detecting it. Indeed, the probability of detection is directly proportional to statistical power. But what does it mean to detect effects? This leads to a question that should be asked in introductory stats course but often isn't...

How do we prove things with statistics?

It would be nice if someone invented a Geiger-counter-type box that you could point at your data and that clicked if there was something there. *Click, click, click—there's a bona fide result in there!*

Better still would be a Starfleet-issued tricorder that could detect evidence of real effects hidden in your database.

Imagine how interesting the Results sections of our papers would be!

Since there are no such effect-detection devices, we have to rely on ancient tools and practices devised by dead statisticians. The most famous of these is the *p* value which has its origins in work done by Sir Ronald Fisher in the 1920s.

Sir Ronald understood that people are very good at looking at the evidence and jumping to the wrong conclusions.

- We pass a white cop who has stopped a black driver and, unaware that the driver has been speeding, we conclude the cop is engaging in racial profiling.
- We notice a colleague arriving late to the office and, unaware that they have just pulled an all-nighter, we assume they are slacking off.
- We ask an overweight friend, "When is the baby due?"

Humans are so good at seeing things that are not there, that we have a name for these sorts of mistakes. We call them Type I errors, a.k.a. false positives, a.k.a. crying wolf.

Sir Ronald wisely decided that researchers need insurance against drawing unsubstantiated conclusions, so he got a hammer and chisel and carved into the proverbial stone the number point-oh-five. If you have ever wondered where the critical p value of .05 comes from, you can thank Fisher (1925).

What does .05 represent? It is the benchmark level of probability we must exceed before we are permitted to draw conclusions from our data. Fisher argued that results which fall below this arbitrary threshold could be considered statistically significant while all others should be viewed with circumspection.

How do we prove things with statistics? You may recall from your Stats 101 course that for every hypothesized effect there is an opposing hypothesis called the null. The null hypothesis is always that the effect size equals zero:

- null hypothesis: there is no effect (the effect size = 0)
- alternative hypothesis: there is some effect (the effect size ≠ 0)

Now this is where it gets a little weird. While we may be interested in, say, the effect of smoking on lung cancer, what we actually test with our stats is something quite different: we test the null. In other words, we test the hypothesis that there is no effect, that smoking *doesn't* cause lung cancer.

Using probability theory, we run statistical tests to determine the likeliness of our result *assuming the null is true*. In other words, if there was no effect, how likely is the result we are seeing? The outcome of this test is the observed probability, the famous *p* value, which decides the fate of our test results (and indirectly, our careers!).

Fisher actually called for researchers to examine different types of evidence when testing hypotheses but history seems to have forgotten that. What we do instead, is bet the farm on the *p*.

For instance, if I find evidence of a link between smoking and lung cancer and the *p* value for my test result is $< .05$, I'll shout, "I found something! Fame and glory, here I come." But if my *p* value $\geq .05$, I'll bang my head against the desk in despair. "There's nothing here! I've wasted the best years of my life on this dud project."

If you think there is something strange about my reaction to the *p* value, you'd be right.

One could argue that the evidence, namely, my estimate of the effect size, stands independently of the *p* value. By focusing on the results of my statistical significance tests, I am missing the really important thing, which is the evidence itself.[1]

Yet such is the state of research that many test results live and die on an arbitrary benchmark set by Fisher. If our test returns a $p < .05$, we stamp our results "statistically significant," pop champagne corks, and tell ourselves, "Congratulations. You found something."

---

[1] Effect sizes are the bread and butter of research. They constitute the evidence of our studies and are the reason why we do what we do. If you are not familiar with effect sizes and how they differ from test statistics like p and t, check out my MadMethods book, *Effect Size Matters.*

Why do Type I errors get all the attention?

You probably learned the difference between Type I and II errors in your first stats course. If you've forgotten, here's a reminder:

- Type I error—seeing things that aren't there
- Type II error—not seeing things that are there

Which error is more embarrassing? According to Sir Ron, Type I errors are the ones to avoid. Far better to skeptically dismiss things that are real than to foolishly accept things that are not.

Since the probability of making either error ranges from 0 (no chance) to 1 (dead certain), Sir Ron decided to set the tolerance level for Type I errors at .05, just a touch above 0. This begs the question, why not set the level of acceptable risk at zero? Why risk *any* Type I errors?

There is a good reason. If we set the cut-off at zero, then none of our results would ever achieve statistical significance and we wouldn't be able to use inferential stats to detect effects.

Setting the cut-off at $p = .00$ is like blinding yourself because you don't want to see cat videos. Now you might have good reasons for disliking cat videos, but I'm sure you would agree that nothing is worth blindness.

It's the same situation here.

If we never risked Type I errors we would make plenty of Type II errors because the two are related. Shut your eyes to avoid Type I errors and you'll invariably make a Type II error. You'll miss things that are worth seeing.

Scientists and researchers are paid to look for things. But if Sir Ron is to be believed, it is better to look with squinty-eyed skepticism than wide-eyed naiveté. "Look, but don't believe everything you see," he might've said. "Cultivate a near-zero tolerance for Type I errors."

Judging by the high esteem held for the mighty *p*, most scholars would agree.

What are four outcomes of any statistical test?

Since there are two types of error—seeing things that aren't there and not seeing things that are—there are four possible outcomes to any test of statistical significance. If there is no effect in the real world, we will either come to the correct conclusion or we will wrongly conclude there is an effect when there isn't (a Type I error). Conversely, if there is an effect, we will either come to the correction conclusion or we will wrongly conclude that there is no effect when there is (a Type II error).

These four outcomes are represented in Figure 1.

You may be wondering about the α and β symbols in the Figure. These Greek letters refer to alpha and beta respectively. Before we jump into power analysis, we need to learn a little bit about both.

I promise you, this will be the only time we do any Greek in this book.

Figure 1: Four test outcomes

	What is true in the real world?	
	There is no effect (null = true)	There is an effect (null = false)
What conclusion is reached? No effect	Correct conclusion ($p = 1 - \alpha$)	Type II error ($p = \beta$)
An effect	Type I error ($p = \alpha$)	Correct conclusion ($p = 1 - \beta$)

What are alpha and beta?

- alpha (α) = the probability of making a Type I error
- beta (β) = the probability of making a Type II error

There, that wasn't too hard was it?

There are two things to note about alpha and beta. First, they are mathematically related. As one goes down the other goes up. So when Sir Ronald says, "I can't bear the thought of making a Type I error," he is implicitly saying, "Type II errors I can live with." He's saying, "I strongly prefer beta to alpha."

The second thing to note about alpha and beta is they are both conditional probabilities; alpha is the conditional probability of making an error *when the null hypothesis is true,* while beta is the conditional probability of making an error *when the null hypothesis is false.*

Which means you are only ever in danger of making one error, not both.

This is one of those things that is so obviously true that many people don't see it. To repeat: the null cannot be true and false at the same time.

Either…

- the null is true (there is no effect) and you cannot make a Type II error, or
- the null is false (there is an effect) and you cannot make a Type I error

Consequently, in any given test only one type of error is possible. You are either risking a Type I error or a Type II error. The problem is we often don't know which error we are risking. When we don't know in advance whether the null is true or false, it is a good idea to insure against both types of error, with most of our insurance going towards errors of the first type.

But what happens when we have prior reasons for believing that an effect really does exist?

Let's say we have years of research testifying to the existence of an effect. In this case it seems pointless insuring against Type I errors since there is no chance—absolutely none at all—of making a Type I error.

The effect *is* real.

The null *is* false.

The only error we can make is a Type II error. The only way we can screw this up is by concluding there is no effect when, in fact, there is.

And how might we make this error? We draw a bad conclusion from a statistically nonsignificant result. This leads to our next question…

What is the wrong way to interpret a statistically nonsignificant result?

A researcher runs a test, gets a statistically nonsignificant result, and concludes, "There is no effect. There is no link, no relationship, no evidence that *X* affects *Y*." This is the wrong way to interpret a nonsignificant result. The absence of evidence is not evidence of absence.

A statistically nonsignificant result is an inconclusive result; it could mean there is no effect, or there is an effect but the test lacked the statistical power to detect it. We can't tell which it is by looking at the *p* value. If there is an effect and you conclude there isn't one, then you've made a Type II error. Publish your result and you'll misdirect future research. It would have been better for all concerned if you had not done the study at all.

As we will see, Type II errors of this type are the bane of the social sciences. They arise because researchers don't know how to distinguish effect sizes from *p* values and because they give no thought to the statistical power of their studies.

The tradeoff between alpha and beta is a big thorny debate that takes us places we don't need to go in this primer. What you do need to know is that while alpha has received all the attention for the past 90–odd years, there is a growing recognition of the need to sensibly manage beta.

This leads us to the next question…

How much power is enough?

Statistical power describes the probability that a test will correctly identify a real effect. (Here we are referring to the box in the lower right corner of Figure 1 above.) How much power should we aim for? If there is an effect to be found, what sort of chance do we want to give ourselves of finding it?

Obviously we would like to have a 100 percent chance of detecting an effect, but to achieve that might require considerable resources.

Imagine you are researching a cure for diabetes and you have developed a promising drug. You want to run a test to find out whether the drug is an effective treatment. One way to know with absolute certainty is to test every diabetes patient on the planet. Give half of them the drug and the rest a placebo in a double-blind trial and then watch what happens.

The beauty of this is approach is that you won't need inferential statistics. Since you are conducting a census instead of relying on a sample, you can simply count heads. If more people recover in the treatment group than the control group, the cure works.

The problem with this approach is it's prohibitively expensive. Close to 400 million people suffer from diabetes. Involving all of them in a trial would not only cost a fortune, it would divert resources away from other potential cures. We ought to be trialing multiple treatments and not betting all our money on just one horse.

So for lots of good reasons we rely on samples and live with a little uncertainty. But how much uncertainty is the right amount? Thanks to Fisher and a century of research practice, we have a rock-solid convention for managing alpha, but what about beta? Is there a conventional level of risk we should be prepared to accommodate when dealing with the threat of Type II errors? There is.

Jacob Cohen (1988) argued that studies should have no more than a 20 percent probability of making a Type II error. Why 20 percent? There's no special reason other than it seems to strike a nice balance between alpha and beta risk. Cohen reasoned that most researchers would view Type I errors as being four times more serious than Type II errors and therefore deserving of more stringent safeguards. Thus, if alpha significance levels are set at .05, then beta levels should be set at .20.

Since statistical power is the probability of detecting an effect when there is an effect to be detected, power can be quantified as the inverse of beta:

$$\text{Statistical power} = 1 - \beta$$

Shooting for a 20 percent risk of beta means designing studies such that they have an 80 percent probability of detecting real effects. Cohen provides the rationale:

> A materially smaller value than .80 would incur too great a risk of a Type II error. A materially larger value would result in a demand for *N* that is likely to exceed the investigator's resources. (Cohen 1992: 156)

Now that we have learned how statistical significance tests are used to make inferences about real world effects, we can finally turn to the analysis of statistical power.

What is power analysis for?

The analysis of statistical power is useful for answering questions like these:

1. How big a sample size do I need to test my hypotheses?
2. I only have access to 40 (or 100 or 15) cases—do I have enough power to test my hypotheses?
3. Assuming the phenomenon I'm searching for is real, what are my chances of finding it given my research design? And how I can increase my chances?

Sticking with our diabetes example, let's say you want to test your drug but you only have access to 40 patients. Is this sample going to be big enough to reveal the effects of your treatment? This is the sort of question that power analysis can answer.

Remember, there are two separate issues here: Either your drug has an effect or it doesn't and either you will conclude that it does or you won't. Each issue requires a different set of skills. The efficacy of your drug will depend on your skills as a drug-maker; the veracity of your conclusions will reflect your skills as a power-analyst.

See the difference?

Power analysis won't help you invent a cure for diabetes. Nor will it help you design an effective strategy, an intervention, a crisis response, an advertising campaign, or any sort of treatment.

But power analysis will help you design and interpret a test which reveals the effectiveness of whatever it is you're testing. It will alert you to the degree of threat posed by a Type II error. And since you have invested resources in what may be a cure for diabetes (or a brilliant strategy, ad-campaign, or whatever), a Type II error is something you definitely don't want to make.

What factors affect statistical power?

Studies vary in their levels of statistical power. Other things equal, a study with a large sample has more power than a study with a small sample. But sample size is just one of four parameters used in power analysis:

1. The **alpha significance criterion** (α) quantifies the risk of committing a Type I error and is conventionally set to a threshold level of .05.

2. The **sample size** or number of observations (N) determines the sampling error and affects the sensitivity of the test. The greater the N the greater the power.

3. The **effect size** (ES) describes the degree to which the phenomenon is present in the population. The larger the effect, the easier it is to detect and the greater the power of the test.

4. **Statistical power** quantifies the chosen Type II error rate (β) and is defined as $1-\beta$. Ideally, the probability of avoiding Type II errors will be at least .80.

How to analyze statistical power and when

The four parameters of power analysis are mathematically related. This means the value of any parameter can be determined from the other three. For instance, if the effect size is small, the sample size is small, and the critical level of alpha is low or stringent, then the resulting power will be low. Why? Because small effects are easy to miss, small samples are more likely to generate sampling errors, and stringent alphas make it harder for researchers to draw conclusions about the effects they may be seeing.

Conversely, if the effect size is big, the sample is large, and the alpha significance criterion is relaxed, statistical power will be high. Why? Because big effects in big samples are easier to see, especially when you're not too worried about the threat of Type I errors.

The relationship between the four parameters of power analysis can be expressed as follows:

$N \rightarrow$ ES $\leftarrow \alpha$ $\uparrow$ Power	If you know the sample size, the desired power and alpha, you can calculate the minimum effect size detectable with your test.
ES $\rightarrow$ N $\leftarrow \alpha$ $\uparrow$ Power	If you know the effect size, the desired power, and the alpha, you can calculate the required sample size.
ES $\rightarrow$ Power $\leftarrow \alpha$ $\uparrow$ N	If you know the effect size, the sample size, and the alpha, you can calculate the statistical power of your test and quantify the threat of Type II errors.

Why are these things good to know?

If you knew prior to conducting a study that you had, at best, only a 20 percent chance of getting a statistically significant result, would you proceed with the study? Or how would you like to know in advance the minimum sample size required to have a decent chance of detecting the effect you are studying? These are the sorts of questions that power analysis can answer.

Consider the following examples:

- If you have a sample of $N = 60$ and anticipate an effect size equivalent to $r = .25$, a quick power calculation would reveal that you have less than a 50 percent chance of obtaining a statistically significant result using a two-tailed test with alpha set at the conventional level of .05. *A 50:50 chance?! I don't like those odds. This project's a dead duck.*

- However, if you were able to double the size of your sample, the probability that your results will turn out to be statistically significant—assuming the effect you're searching for actually exists—rises to nearly 80 percent. *Oh, that's much better. I'm sure I can get the extra funding I need to keep this project alive.*

Now we begin to understand why Cohen said he felt like he had died and gone to heaven when he stumbled on to power analysis. It's like getting a crystal ball and determining whether your results are going to pan out *before you've begun the study!*

When is the best time to do a power analysis?

Ideally, a power analysis should be run before a study is conducted. Such an analysis is prospective in nature. Its purpose is to help us make informed judgments before we commit resources to a new project.

Prospective analyses of statistical power can be used to determine minimum detectable effect sizes, required sample sizes, and the likelihood of making Type II errors given other factors. Let's see how this works in practice with reference to our diabetes drug example…

How do I calculate the minimum detectable effect size?

We have 40 patients, we decide to follow convention and set alpha at .05, and we agree with Cohen that 0.80 is a desirable level of statistical power (meaning, we are prepared to tolerate, at worst, a 20 percent chance of making a Type II error). Given these three parameters, what is the smallest effect size we will be able to detect in our study?

Effects come in two families; the *d*-family and the *r*-family. Since in this study we are likely to be comparing a treatment group with a control group (with 20 in each group), we will measure effects using metrics from the *d*-family.

To calculate the minimum effect size, we might consult a table such as Table 1:

Table 1: Minimum detectable effect sizes

	d		*r*	
Sample size	One-tailed	Two-tailed	One-tailed	Two-tailed
10	1.72	2.02	.70	.76
20	1.16	1.32	.53	.58
30	.93	1.06	.44	.48
40	.80	.91	.38	.43
50	.71	.81	.34	.38
60	.65	.74	.31	.35
70	.60	.68	.29	.33
80	.56	.63	.27	.31
90	.53	.60	.26	.29
100	.50	.57	.25	.28

Source: Adapted from Ellis (2010b, Table 3.2).
Note: alpha = .05, power = .80

This table tells us that for a pooled sample size of 40 patients, the minimum detectable effect size in the *d* metric when using two-tailed tests is .91. This is a huge effect size. To put it in context, the effect of the beta-blocker propranolol on survival rates for heart attacks is a much smaller $d = .08$ (Kolata 1981).

What does this mean? Our power analysis reveals that unless we have some fantastic wonder-drug on our hands, any results we get are unlikely to achieve statistical significance. Sadly, we doubt that our drug is a miracle cure. In fact, we have good reasons to suspect its effect might be rather small.

(Most effects are small. Small doesn't necessarily mean trivial since small effects may lead to noteworthy improvements in health or add up to large consequences.)

If we are dealing with a small effect, a sample size of 40 is not going to be much use. By that I mean, a small effect is unlikely to register as statistically significant because our study lacks power. Okay. So assuming the effect *is* small, how big a sample would we need? This leads us to our next question…

How do I calculate the required sample size?

Based on the evidence of past research we have good reasons to anticipate an effect size of *d* = .20. To calculate the minimum sample size needed to detect such an effect given conventional levels of alpha and power, we might consult a table such as Table 2. The left-hand columns of the table show us the minimum sample sizes required for a range of effect sizes in the *d* metric; the right-hand columns provide sample sizes for a range of effect sizes in the *r* metric.

Table 2: Minimum sample sizes

ES = *d*	N	ES = *r*	N
.10	3,142	.05	3,137
.20	787	.10	782
.30	351	.15	346
.40	199	.20	193
.50	128	.25	123
.60	90	.30	84
.70	67	.35	61
.80	52	.40	46
.90	41	.45	36
1.00	34	.50	29

Source: Adapted from Ellis (2010b, Table 3.1).
Notes: The sample sizes reported for *d* are pooled (i.e., $n_1 + n_2$), α_2 =.05, power = .80

Table 2 tells is that for an effect size equivalent to d = 0.2, we will need a sample size of at least N = 787 to have an 80 percent chance of detection (or a 20 percent chance of avoiding a Type II error).

In other words, to detect a small effect you need a big sample.[2]

And if you plan on doing subgroup or multivariate analyses, you'll need a bigger sample still.

Minimum sample sizes should be based on the size of the smallest group to be tested or on the number of predictors in your model.[3]

---

[2] If you decide to verify these numbers with a computer program such as G*Power 3, you will get a minimum sample size of 788, not 787. Which is correct? They both are. The sample sizes in Table 2 are pooled, meaning, you have to cut them in half to figure out how many in each of your comparison groups. Half of 787 is 393.5. Since you can't put 393.5 people into a group, the safe bet is to round up and have 394. If you have two groups of 394, your combined sample size is 788, which is the number that G*Power 3 gives you.

[3] Since it is beyond the scope of this short guide to delve into these issues, the interested reader is directed to Green (1991) and Kelley and Maxwell (2008).

How do I calculate the statistical power of my study?

Clearly, 40 patients isn't going to cut it. If we proceed with such a small sample the probability of making a Type II error runs as high as 91 percent. Continue with the study as is, and we are setting ourselves up for almost certain failure (if by "fail" we mean fail to reach a conclusive result).

Wait, slow down.

How did I arrive at this figure of 91 percent?

On this occasion, I didn't consult a table but I used a program called G*Power 3. Figure 2 provides a screenshot.

This program is a powerful tool suited to running a variety of power analyses. You can download it for free from a site maintained by the University of Dusseldorf (see Faul *et al.*, 2007, 2009).

Figure 2: Calculating power with G*Power 3

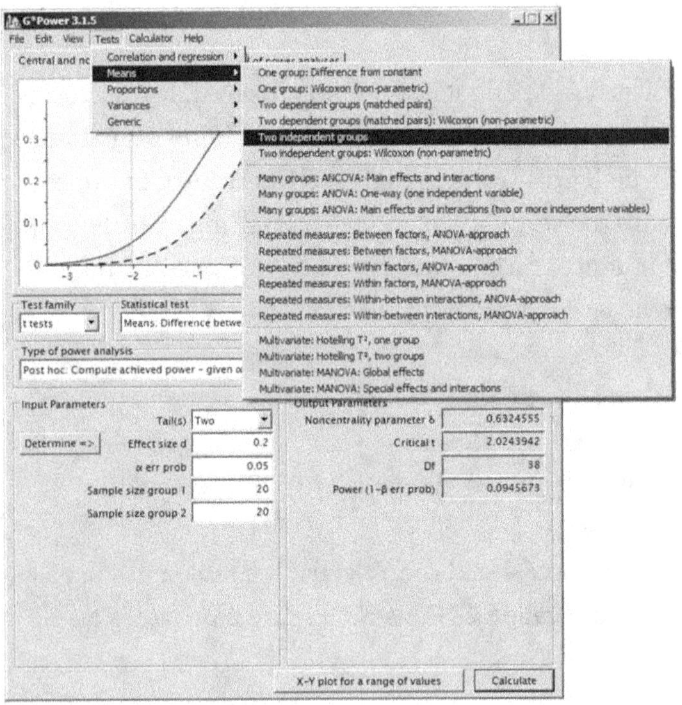

To learn how G*Power 3 works, download the free user-guide when you install the program, but here are the steps I followed to determine the likelihood of a Type II error in our diabetes example:

1. From the menu bar at the top of the app I selected Tests>Means>Two independent groups

2. Under "Type of Power Analysis," I selected "Post hoc"

3. I inputted the following parameters:
   - for "Tail(s)" I entered two (indicating a two-tailed test)
   - for "Effect size d" I entered 0.2
   - I left the "α err prob" unchanged at 0.05
   - for "Sample size group 1" I entered 20 and I did the same for "Sample size group 2"

4. I then pressed "Calculate" and got the numbers you see in the screenshot

The number of interest is found in the box on the lower right-hand corner:

$$\text{Power } (1-\beta \text{ err prob}) = 0.0945673$$

This is the power of our study. Since power equals 1 - β, then beta (the probability of making a Type II error) equals 1 - 0.0945673 or 0.91.

So far all our examples have been in the *d* metric, but what if we wanted to run power analyses for effects measured in the correlational or *r* metric? It's the same basic process. The tables above along with those you'll find in power texts generally provide two sets of figures, one for each metric. As long as you can tell d from r you won't have any problems. Similarly, G*Power 3 provides the full gamut of tests for the r metric. Here's a worked example…

How do I calculate sample size using G*Power 3?

Say you want to do a study assessing the link between exposure to tobacco smoke and the risk of lung cancer. You have reason to believe that the correlation between these two variables is equivalent to $r = .30$. (How do you know this? You did a meta-analysis or ran a pre-test.) How big a sample would you need to test for an effect of this size?

1. From the menu bar at the top of G*Power 3 select Tests>Correlation and regression>Correlation: bivariate normal model

2. Under "Type of Power Analysis" select "A priori: Compute required sample size"

3. Input the following parameters:

- for "Tail(s)" enter two (indicating a two-tailed test)
- for "Correlation ϱ H1" enter 0.3
- leave "α err prob" unchanged at 0.05
- for Power ($1-\beta$ err prob) enter 0.8
- leave "Correlation ϱ H0" unchanged at 0 (this is the null hypothesis)

4. Press "Calculate" and you should end up with the numbers you see in the screenshot shown in Figure 3.

The output of interest is in the cell marked "Total sample size." The result tells us that we need a minimum sample size of $N = 84$ if we are to have an 80 percent probability of detecting an effect size equivalent to $r = 0.3$. (Just for fun, you can cross-check these numbers with Table 2 above.)

But what if we decided to run a directional or one-tailed test instead? After all, there is considerable evidence to show that exposure to tobacco smoke has an adverse effect on lung health. There is not a lot of debate over the direction of the effect. Smoking doesn't make you healthy.

Figure 3: Calculating sample size with G*Power 3

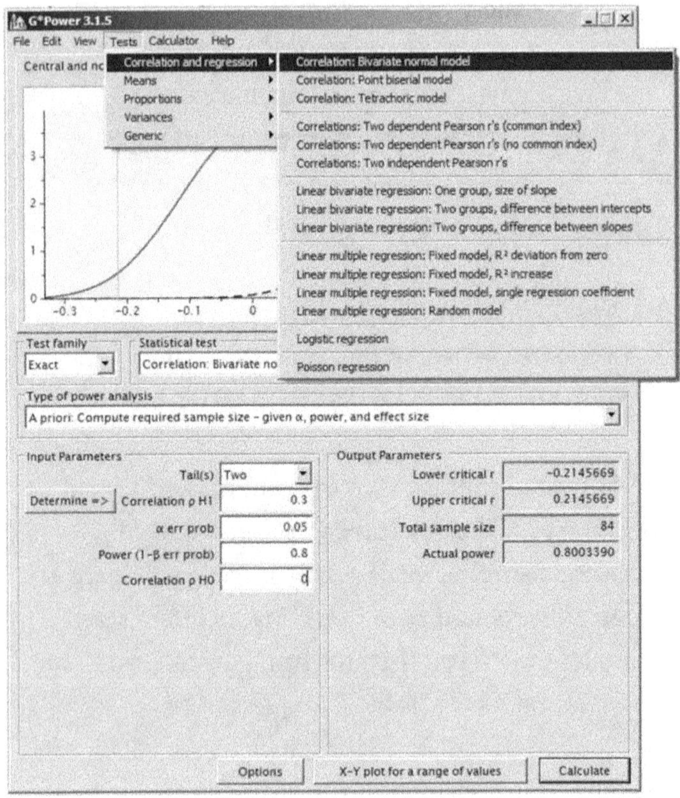

In this case we could rerun the analysis after selecting "One" in the box next to "Tails." Switching from a two-tailed to a one-tailed test boosts statistical power as evidenced by a corresponding drop in the required sample size. This time we only need $N = 67$ to achieve the same level of power as before.

Clear as mud?

If you would like a little more practice analyzing statistical power or calculating sample sizes, check out the bonus exercises in Appendix 1.

Why are most effects small?

In the examples we've just done, we have had a prior expectation about the size of the effect, but in practice, we often have no idea. We're in the dark. If you don't know the size of the effect you are looking for, set your expectations low. Chances are, it's small. Really small.

Why do I say this?

Results are like gold nuggets—the big ones get picked up first. The pioneers in any new field of inquiry get to pluck the low-hanging fruit. What remains for those who follow are the crumbs. (I hope you like mixed metaphors!)

For a long time I had a nagging suspicion that the majority of effects in the social sciences are small. However, when I looked at the evidence in my own field, I was amazed to find that the majority of effects are actually smaller than small—they're tiny.

Here's how I came to that conclusion.

Wanting to identify some typical effect sizes in the field of international business, I scanned 32 journals to identify every meta-analysis published in a 15–year period.[4] My search led to the identification of 23 meta-analyses that collectively accounted for a combined sample of $N = 223{,}800$ (see Ellis 2010a).

Here is what I found: Of the 23 mean effect sizes reported in the meta-analyses,

- five would be regarded as small in terms of Cohen's (1992) effect size conventions (i.e., $.10 \leq r < .30$)
- eighteen would be regarded as smaller than small (i.e., $r < .10$)

Figure 4 portrays the 23 mean effect sizes graphically. It should be obvious from this figure that typical effect sizes in international business are not very big.

---

[4] What is a meta-analysis? A meta-analysis is where you pool the results of available research to calculate a weighted, mean estimate of effect size. A meta-analysis can help you identify the effect size you need to run a power analysis. Conducting a meta-analysis is not hard. As I explain in my MadMethods book, *Meta-Analysis Made Easy*, you can learn the basics in less than an hour.

In fact, the weighted mean of the 23 weighted mean effect sizes was just $r = .06$. That is tiny, some might say, even trivial in size.

In percentage of variance terms it means that the average effect size is equivalent to less than half of one percent.

International business researchers have it tough!

These results are not unusual. Meta-analyses done in other social science disciplines routinely report effect sizes that are small in size (e.g., Mazen *et al.*, 1987).

We all have it tough!

What do we do with this information?

The best response is make sure our studies are sufficiently empowered to detect small effects.

Figure 4: Mean effect sizes in international business research

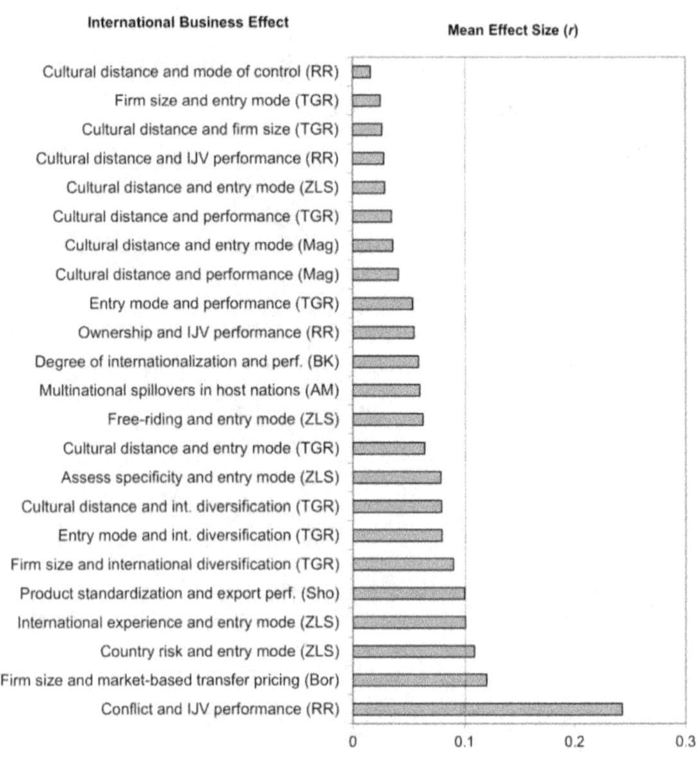

Notes: Effect sizes are expressed in absolute values. AM = Abumustafa and Mohamed (2009), BK = Bausch and Krist (2007), Bor = Borkowski (1996), Mag = Magnusson, *et al.*, (2008), RR = Reus and Rottig (2009), Sho = Shoham (2003), TGR = Tihanyi, Griffith and Russell (2005), ZLS = Zhao, Luo and Suh (2004)

Say the effect you are searching for is equivalent to $r = .06$. Under conventional levels of alpha and power, you will need a sample size of at least 2,177 to detect such a small effect. If you decide to relax your statistical significance standards by opting for one-tailed rather than two-tailed tests, you will still need an N of at least 1,716 to give yourself an 80 percent chance of getting a statistically significant result.

These are big sample sizes, bigger, I suspect, than the majority of those found in the social sciences. This leads to our next question…

The dangers of an under-powered study

Hopefully by now the answer to this question is obvious. The lower the power, the greater the probability you won't find anything. Or rather, the greater the likelihood you'll get an inconclusive result.

There is a two-fold risk here. First, in any low-powered study, the estimate of the effect size is likely to be tainted by sampling error. How can you be sure that your small sample is not quirky in some unpredictable way? There is a reason pollsters survey thousands rather than dozens of people, and that is to reduce the margin of error in their results.

Second, if your study lacks statistical power, there is a greater chance of making a Type II error. This happens because the smaller your sample, the greater the likelihood that your results will turn out to be statistically nonsignificant. A nonsignificant result is *not* a Type II error but it can lead to one.

How does low statistical power lead to Type II errors?

This point is worth repeating: Low power leads to statistically nonsignificant results and a nonsignificant result is an *inconclusive* result. It might mean there is no effect, or there is an effect but the test lacked the statistical power to detect it.

If you interpret a statistically nonsignificant result as evidence of no effect, and there really is an effect, then you will have made a Type II error.

My study is under-powered, how can I increase statistical power?

As we will see in Part B, most studies done are woefully under-powered. They lack the power to detect sought-after effects and so run a high risk of generating Type II errors. In many cases there is a clear need for more power. How can we get it? Here are five ways:

1. Increase the sample size

The size of your sample will likely have the biggest effect on the statistical power of your study. So to increase power, increase *N*. In some cases doubling the *N* will lead to a greater than doubling of statistical power, but not always. In a few situations increasing the *N* will have only a marginal effect on statistical power. The point is not to throw money at the problem but to determine your ideal sample size by analyzing the trade-off between sampling costs, which are additive, and the corresponding gains in power, which may be incremental and diminishing.

2. Search for bigger effects

Tighter relationships are easier to spot than mediated or moderated relationships, so one way to increase power is to look for outcomes that are closely related to treatments (or dependent variables that are closely related to predictors).

3. Reduce measurement error

Unreliable measures are like dirty lenses on telescopes—they make it harder to see what you're looking for.

It is beyond the scope of this short book to examine the relationship between measurement error and statistical power but it's not a happy one.

Measurement error is like a leech sucking the power out of your study.[5]

4. Choose appropriate statistical tests for the data

Parametric tests are more powerful than non-parametric tests; directional (one-tailed) tests are more powerful than non-directional (two-tailed) tests; and tests involving metric data are more powerful than tests involving nominal or ordinal data.

5. Relax the alpha significance criterion (α)

Take a hammer and smash those stone tablets of Fisher's. Yes, you will run into institutional opposition—the .05 is held sacred by many. But a thoughtful researcher should be able to make a good argument for relaxing alpha in settings where the risk of a Type II error is greater than the risk of a Type I error. It won't be easy to convince reviewers, but you could try.

---

[5] To learn more about the leech and how to kill it, see Ellis 2010b, chapter 3.

The dangers of an over-powered study

Hopefully it is clear by now that under-powered studies are generally not worth doing. If there isn't a good chance of finding what you're looking for, why waste resources looking for it? The temptation then might be to pursue as much power as possible. But over-powered studies are not without dangers of their own.

Consider a study with a sample size of 5,000. Without running a power analysis we can safely conclude that such a study has tons of power and it does. In fact, it will be powerful enough to detect effects as small as $r = .04$. The question is, are such effects worth detecting? In some settings they might be, but most of the time effects of this size are rightly dismissed as trivial, barely real, and possibly reflecting nothing more than background noise in the database.

I recently came across a study in a top tier journal that was based on a panel dataset of 117,000 observations. The results table looked like a conference for asterisks. Or a map of the night sky. Not only was everything statistically significant, but most results were significant at the $p < .01$ level. It was quite a sight.

Now there is nothing wrong with having lots of statistically significant results. The problem was the authors interpreted all of their results as though they were *practically* significant. In other words, they confused statistical with substantive significance. Such is the mindless adherence to the sacred .05 that none of the reviewers picked this up.

If these authors had examined their effect sizes directly, they would have dismissed a lot of their statistically significant results as trivial. For instance, one of their results was so small that it in proportion of variance terms the predictor accounted for $1/25^{th}$ of one percent of the variance in the outcome variable. That's what you call a nothing effect. It's the weight of your shadow. It's the sound of an eyelid closing. However, distracted by their rash of asterisks (indicating low p values), the authors missed the utter trivialness of this effect and interpreted the test result as evidence in support of their hypothesis. It wasn't.

To clarify, the problem is not one of having too much data—the more the better!—but in the possibly prodigal expenditure of resources. A study is wasteful to the degree to which the costs of collecting the data needed to estimate effects exceed the benefits of doing so.[6]

Why can't I draw substantive conclusions from *p* values?

It is not uncommon for researchers to draw conclusions about observed effects by examining *p* values generated by tests of significance. If a result is statistically significant, unwise authors will conclude conclude that the effect is real, big, and interesting.

---

[6] The use of secondary or published data can lead to samples that are phenomenally huge, such as Singh's (2007) analysis of 6.9m patent dyads. Another interesting trend is the growing number of studies done in China where large numbers seem to be the name of the game. The largest study based on primary data that I have come across is Hung *et al.*,'s (2007) analysis of market segments and consumer behavior in China. Their second sample (N = 32,670) drew on data obtained from a mix of interviews and self-administered surveys. Coincidentally, their study was published in the same issue as Singh's (2007) large N study making volume 38, issue 5 of the *Journal of International Business Studies* arguably the most statistically powerful journal issue of all time.

However, none of these conclusions is supported by the *p* value.

The *p* value is a confounded index. It changes in relation to the effect size *and* the sample size. If either one goes up *p* goes down. In many studies the biggest determinant of statistical power is sample size. Consequently, a *p* value usually says less about the size of the effect than the size of the sample from which it came.

Draw your conclusions from *p* values and you'll either risk missing small effects obtained in low-power settings (leading to a Type II error) or you'll make too much of trivial effects observed in high-power settings (leading to a Type I error). The best way to avoid either outcome is to interpret effect sizes independently of statistical significance tests.

My study is highly-powered, how can I avoid the dangers of misinterpretation?

Simple—don't draw substantive conclusions from *p* values. Instead, look at your estimate of the effect size and answer two questions: How big is it? And what does it mean?

Interpreting statistical significance is easy; interpreting substantive significance is a different game entirely and one that requires you to think, to compare your estimates with those obtained from other studies, and to contextualize your results against a meaningful frame of reference.[7]

What is the tricky part of doing a power analysis?

If you are running a prospective power analysis, you're probably doing it because you want to know the required sample size. What's the catch? To calculate the sample size you need to know the effect size and that's probably the one thing you *don't* know (else why are you doing the study?).

It's a catch-22 situation: You can't design a good study without knowing the likely effect size and you can't know the effect size until you've done a good study!

Nor is this something you can afford to get wrong. Under-estimate the likely effect size and you will

---

[7] I provide tips and tricks on how to deal with the interpretation challenge in my MadMethods book *Effect Size Matters.*

over-state the required sample size, possibly to the point of killing the project. *We need how big a sample?! We can't afford that.* But over-estimate the effect size and the study may be under-powered and doomed to fail.

For these reasons it is essential that you have a fair idea of the expected effect size *before* you commit to a study. If you don't know how big the thing is that you're looking for, you won't know how much power you need to find it.

So where can you get good information on the likely effect size? You have three options:

1. refer to evidence of effect sizes reported in past research
2. make an estimate of the effect size based on theory
3. conduct a pre-test

A pre-test is always good idea, particularly if you plan on applying for a big research grant further down the track.

In our diabetes example we already have a sample of 40 patients ready to go. As we have seen, this sample size is not big enough to give us the definitive answers we are looking for. But if we use this group for a pre-test, we could learn plenty that will help us later on.

Here's how that could work.

We split the sample into two groups—a treatment group and a control group—and test our new drug. We measure the health of each group before and after the treatment and discover an improvement in the treatment group equivalent to $d = 0.55$. Unsurprisingly, a *t*-test reveals this result to be statistically nonsignificant.

Here's the wrong way to interpret that information:

Since our *t*-test revealed that the treatment had a statistically nonsignificant effect, we conclude the treatment doesn't work.

Why is that the wrong way? Because we don't know that the treatment doesn't work. All we know for sure is that with only 40 patients our study was never going to be capable of detecting anything less than whopper-sized effects. If our study has given us an accurate estimate of the effect size, we've just made a Type II error and the one thing we should have known in advance was that the chances of that happening were high (60 percent, to be precise).

So what is the right way to interpret this result?

Our pretest revealed an improvement in the treatment group equivalent to $d = 0.55$ which we interpret as promising and worthy of further investigation. Based on estimates reporting in previous research, we anticipate the likely effect size to be in the 0.45–0.65 range. Thus, we intend to seek funding for a larger study (*N* at least 158) to further test this treatment.

Same data, different conclusions. Go with the first conclusion and you'll kill a promising new drug. Go with the second conclusion and you may end up helping 400 million diabetes patients. You could win a Nobel Prize!

Is it too much of an exaggeration to say that the course and success of your career hinges on your ability to analyze statistical power?

What's wrong with retrospective power analyses?

So far we have looked at the situation where a power analysis is used to inform the design of future studies. But what about doing a power analysis after the fact?

Say you do a study and get a bunch of statistically nonsignificant results. You wonder, "What went wrong? Perhaps my study lacked power. Let's crunch the numbers to find out."

Beware! You are on the top of a slippery slope.

What is wrong with calculating power retrospect-ively? After all, isn't it reasonable to ask questions like:

- "My sample was too small; how big should it have been?"
- "Was insufficient power responsible for my nonsignificant result?"
- "What was the probability of making a Type II error in this study?"

These are fair questions and sometimes you will encounter journal editors who ask them. But calculating the power of a study based on the parameters of that study is fraught with danger.

The problem is this: observed effect sizes drawn from individual samples (especially small samples characterized by sampling error) are likely to be poor estimates of actual effect sizes. If you were to take the effect size estimate from your study and plug it into a retrospective power analysis, it would tell you nothing you didn't know and it would likely mislead you.

"But I got a statistically nonsignificant result," you might say. "I can't tell whether that means there is no effect or there is but my study lacked the power to detect it."

Again, this is a valid concern but a retrospective power analysis cannot help you resolve it. Take another look at Figure 1 above. Statistical power is only relevant in the right side of the table. It is only applies when the null is false. To calculate power after the fact is to make an assumption—the null is false—that is unsupported by the data. It's like trying to calculate an equation with two unknowns (Zumbo and Hubley 1998).

But what if we qualified our thoughts like this:

> I am going to assume the effect is real (or the null is false) because other research says so. I am further going to assume the effect size is the same as what I observed in my study. Under these circumstances, how big should my sample size have been given conventional levels of alpha and power?

There is nothing wrong with this question because it is prospective in nature. It is exactly the sort of question we might ask after a pre-test. Whether a power analysis based on these assumptions will generate good results or not hinges on how closely the effect size observed in the study reflects the true population effect size.

Intermission

In Part A we concerned ourselves with the basics of power analysis—why, how, and when to do it. Designing studies with statistical power in mind is one of the best ways to ensure research success.

So far we have limited our focus to the design of single studies. But researchers sometimes assess the statistical power of entire fields of study. They do this to gauge the prevalence of Type II errors and otherwise assess the statistical health of specific fields.

In Part B we will see that the results of these power surveys routinely reveal fatal flaws in published research.

The really bad news of power research

In the 1960s, Jacob Cohen had a brilliant idea: Why not calculate the average statistical power of all the studies published in the 1960 volume of *The Journal of Abnormal and Social Psychology*?

I know, it's a zinger of an idea. You're probably wondering, "Why didn't I think of that?"

Seriously, Cohen's idea was profoundly clever for it meant he could quantify, in cold, hard numbers, the prevalence of Type II errors in his field.

How did he do it?

Cohen recorded the sample sizes and test types for all 70 studies published in the 1960 volume and calculated average power for three hypothetical effect sizes. He found that the average power for detecting small, medium, and large effects was 0.18, 0.48, and 0.83 respectively.

These numbers are startling.

They tell us that unless the effects researchers were looking for were large, they had a greater chance of making a Type II error than getting a statistically significant result.

In other words, the majority of studies published in the 1960 volume of *The Journal of Abnormal and Social Psychology* were designed to be inconclusive.

Cohen's (1962) study was brilliant in its simplicity and stunning in its conclusions.

Almost immediately others started using his methods to calculate average power levels in fields such as education (Brewer 1972), communication (Kroll and Chase 1975), social work (Orme and Combs-Orme 1986), marketing research (Sawyer and Ball 1981), management (Mazen *et al.*, 1987), counseling research (Kosciulek and Szymanski 1993), and behavioral accounting (Borkowski *et al.*, 2001).

Following Cohen's lead, many of these surveys were limited to specific journals.

Which journals have had their statistical power assessed?

Power analysts have attempted to gauge the average power of research published in the following 25 journals;

- Academy of Management Journal (Brock 2003; Cashen and Geiger 2004; Mazen *et al.*, 1987)
- Accounting Review (Lindsay 1993)
- Administrative Science Quarterly (Cashen and Geiger 2004; Mone *et al.*, 1996)
- American Educational Research Journal (Brewer 1972)
- Behavioral Research in Accounting (Borkowski *et al.*, 2001)
- British Journal of Psychology (Clark-Carter 1997)
- Decision Sciences (Baroudi and Orlikowski 1989)
- Journal of Abnormal Psychology (Rossi 1990)
- Journal of Abnormal and Social Psychology (Cohen 1962; Sedlmeier and Gigerenzer 1989)
- Journal of Accounting Research (Lindsay 1993)
- Journal of Applied Psychology (Chase and Chase 1976; Mone *et al.*, 1996)
- Journal of Clinical and Experimental Neuropsychology (Bezeau and Graves 2001)

- Journal of Consulting and Clinical Psychology (Rossi 1990)
- Journal of Information Systems (McSwain 2004)
- Journal of International Business Studies (Brock 2003; Ellis 2010a)
- Journal of Management (Cashen and Geiger 2004; Mazen *et al.*, 1987; Mone *et al.*, 1996)
- Journal of Management Accounting (Borkowski *et al.*, 2001)
- Journal of Management Information Systems (McSwain 2004)
- Journal of Management Studies (Cashen and Geiger 2004)
- Journal of Marketing Research (Sawyer and Ball 1981)
- Journal of Personality and Social Psychology (Rossi 1990)
- Management Sciences (Baroudi and Orlikowski 1989)
- MIS Quarterly (Baroudi and Orlikowski 1989)
- Neuropsychology (Bezeau and Graves 2001)
- Strategic Management Journal (Brock 2003; Cashen and Geiger 2004; Mone *et al.*, 1996)

The unanimous and overwhelming conclusion of these power surveys is that research across all social science disciplines is woefully underpowered. The typical study published in these journals lacked the power to detect anything except the largest of effect sizes (Ellis 2010b, Table 4.1). Since large effects are as rare as hen's teeth, the implications of this are sobering.

First, low power translates into an increased prevalence of Type II errors. Many studies are likely to be missing real effects simply because they lack the power to detect them.

Second, and somewhat surprisingly, low power across disciplines also translates into an increased prevalence of Type I errors. Not only are researchers missing things, they are seeing things that are not there. Consider these two contrasting facts:

- with low average statistical power, the typical study in the social sciences has a small chance of finding anything
- yet most published studies have found something, otherwise they would not have been published

How is this possible?

How is it that so many published studies have found something given that the odds of doing so were stacked against them?

There are two possible explanations. Either published studies routinely detect large effects (they don't) or authors of published studies are mistaking random variation in their samples for genuine effects (gulp!).

How does low statistical power lead to Type I errors?

In Part A we saw how low statistical power can lead to Type II errors. With insufficient power, you miss things. That much is obvious. But when low power is combined with publication policies favoring studies that find things over studies that don't, the paradoxical result is an increase in Type I errors.

How does this happen?

Recall that studies are purposely designed to balance the competing risks of Type I and Type II errors. Under normal circumstances this means that a small percentage of false positives is inevitable. In fact, for any set of studies about one in sixteen will be affected by Type I errors. That is, they will find things that don't exist.[8]

However, as average power levels fall, the proportion of false positives reported and published inevitably rises.

This happens because researchers sometimes fish in the data and engage in the sin of HARKing.

---

[8] These numbers are explained in Ellis 2010b, chapter 4.

What is HARKing? And is it contagious?

HARKing, or Hypothesizing After the Results are Known, is what you do when you stumble upon an unexpected result and then write the paper as if that result was your study's original object (Kerr 1998).

What's wrong with HARKing or fishing in the data?

The problem is your result is probably not real; it's a statistical fluke, an aberration in your sample. Run a large enough number of tests and the odds are good that something will turn out to be statistically significant, even if there's nothing there.

Imagine you've spent three long years on a study, crunched your numbers, and found… nothing. It's depressing. The temptation to play with the data is almost overwhelming. *There must be something here. I must find something to show for my labors.*

Well, run enough tests and you will find something. The probabilistic nature of null hypothesis signif-

icance testing guarantees that *something* will eventually turn out to be statistically significant even if there is *nothing* there.
So you play with the data, find a statistically significant result, and write a paper about it. "It must be real right? The *p* value says so." Wrong! What you have found is probably little more than a sampling quirk. You have a bona fide false positive. If you tried to replicate the result in a follow-up study, you would probably find that it did not exist.

But there's no time for that. It's publish or perish, up or out. So you write a compelling paper, fool a reviewer or two, and get a hit. Congratulations, you've just done bad science. You've reported something that's not real and misdirected future research on the topic.

For these reasons some scholars suspect that published results are more often wrong than right (e.g., Ioannidis 2005).

How can I avoid the temptation to HARK?

Rewriting papers to suit unexpected findings is a temptation some are unable to resist. How can we protect ourselves from the temptation to engage in a little bit of HARKing? What steps can we take to ensure we don't engage in this sort of bad science? There are at four things you can do:

1. Design studies with adequate levels of power—not too little (or you won't see anything) or too much (or you will see everything; effects, quirks, sampling errors, random noise).

2. Don't fish in the dataset. Just don't. Let theory be your guide.

3. If you do stumble upon an unexpected result, label it as such—don't try and tell yourself that this is what you were looking for all along. Let others know that the result is unexpected and possibly dubious.

4. Validate your results through replication.

The main takeaway from this book

In this book we have learned that the majority of studies in the social sciences are fatally flawed by design, meaning, they are under-powered and unlikely to detect effects of interest. We have looked at five ways for increasing statistical power and we have discussed simple methods for computing minimum sample sizes and detectable effects. We have also learned why you cannot draw substantive conclusions from p values and why fishing in your dataset is a bad idea.

If I was to distill the single most important lesson of this book, it would be this: Consider statistical power when designing studies and running tests.

Studies which have too much or too little statistical power are inherently wasteful and potentially misleading. Even if researchers are careful to avoid making Type II errors, any underpowered study will lead to an inconclusive and therefore unsatisfactory result. For this reason the *Publication Manual* of the American Psychological Association makes the following recommendation:

> When applying inferential statistics, take seriously the statistical power considerations associated with tests of the hypotheses. Such considerations relate to the likelihood of correctly rejecting the tested hypotheses, given a particular alpha level, effect size, and sample size. In that regard, routinely provide evidence that the study has sufficient power to detect effects of substantive interest. (APA 2010: 30)

"Provide evidence of sufficient power." Evidence in this context would be a prospective analysis of statistical power based on the anticipated effect size.

Prior expectations regarding the effect size should be informed either by theory or past research (including pre-tests) rather than effect sizes observed in the study itself. When researchers have little choice but to rely on small samples, statistical power considerations should motivate them to seek out large effects.

As we have seen, analyzing statistical power is not difficult. Anyone who can run a statistical test should be able to do a power analysis. Neither is power analysis time-consuming. Usually no more than an hour is needed. Given the potential benefits of analyzing power prior to starting projects that may run for years, it is an hour well spent.

Author's note

If you enjoyed *Statistical Power Trip,* would you mind posting a short customer review on Amazon? Doing so will help others find this book.

Thank you!

Appendix I: Bonus power exercises

Use either G*Power 3 or Tables 1 and 2 in this book to…

(a) calculate the required sample sizes for the following test conditions:

	ES metric	Effect size	Sample size
1.	*d*	0.60	
2.	*d*	0.10	
3.	*d*	0.70	
4.	*d*	0.40	
5.	*d*	0.30	
6.	*r*	0.45	
7.	*r*	0.05	
8.	*r*	0.20	
9.	*r*	0.25	
10.	*r*	0.10	

Note: alpha = .05, power = .80, all tests are two-tailed

(b) calculate the minimum detectable effect size for the following test conditions:

	Sample size	Test type	ES metric	Minimum detectable effect size
1.	80	1–tailed	*d*	
2.	20	1–tailed	*d*	
3.	50	2–tailed	*r*	
4.	100	1–tailed	*r*	
5.	40	2–tailed	*d*	
6.	90	2–tailed	*r*	
7.	60	1–tailed	*d*	
8.	10	2–tailed	*r*	
9.	30	2–tailed	*r*	
10.	70	2–tailed	*d*	

Note: alpha = .05, power = .80

Answers are on the following page.

Answers to exercises on the preceding page:

Exercise (a): (1) 90, (2) 3,142, (3) 67, (4) 199, (5) 351, (6) 36, (7) 3,137, (8) 193, (9) 123, (10) 782.
Exercise (b): (1) .56, (2) 1.16, (3) .38, (4) .25, (5) .91, (6) .29, (7) .65, (8) .76, (9) .48, (10) .68.

Note: Sample sizes for *d* are pooled (i.e., $n_1 + n_2$). When implementing the results of exercise (a) in the context of group comparisons, sample sizes with odd numbers should be rounded up to the nearest even number to permit equal numbers within each group.

Appendix 2: Ten great but slightly misquoted quotes about statistical power

"The measure of a man is what he does with *statistical* power."

— Plato (424BC–348BC), Greek number cruncher

"An honest man can feel no pleasure in the exercise of *statistical* power over his fellow citizens."

— Thomas Jefferson (1743–1826), third US President

"Only a man who knows what it is like to be defeated can reach down to the bottom of his soul and come up with the extra ounce of *statistical* power it takes to win when the match is even."

— Muhammad Ali (1942–2016), professional boxer and *Sports Illustrated*'s Sportsman of the Century

"All things are subject to interpretation; whichever interpretation prevails at a given time is a function of *statistical* power and not truth."

— Friedrich Nietzsche (1844–1900) German philosopher

"The day the power of love overrules the love of *statistical* power, the world will know peace."

— Mahatma Gandhi (1869–1948)
leader of Indian independence movement

"Being *statistically* powerful is like being a lady. If you have to tell people you are, you aren't."

— Margaret Thatcher (1925–2013)
Britain's first female prime minister

"Nearly all men can stand adversity, but if you want to test a man's character, give him *statistical* power."

— Abraham Lincoln (1809–1865)
sixteenth US President

"*Statistical* power is the ultimate aphrodisiac."

— Henry Kissinger (1923–)
former US Secretary of State

"*Statistical* power is my mistress. I have worked too hard at her conquest to allow anyone to take her away from me."

— Napoleon Bonaparte (1769–1821), French Emperor

"With great *statistical* power, comes great responsibility."

— Ben Parker, Spiderman's uncle

References

Abumustafa, N.I., and M.M. Mohamed (2009), "Do domestic firms benefit from multinational enterprises? A meta-analysis of the empirical research," *Journal of Transnational Management*, 14(1): 3–15.

APA (2010), Publication Manual of the American Psychological Association, 6th Edition. Washington DC: American Psychological Association.

Baroudi, J.J. and W.J. Orlikowski (1989), "The problem of statistical power in MIS research," *MIS Quarterly*, 13(1): 87–106.

Bausch, A., and M. Krist (2007), "The effect of context-related moderators on the internationalization-performance relationship: Evidence from meta-analysis," *Management International Review*, 47(3): 319–347.

Bezeau, S. and R. Graves (2001), "Statistical power and effect sizes of clinical neuropsychology research," *Journal of Clinical and Experimental Neuropsychology*, 23(3): 399–406.

Borkowski, S.C. (1996), "An analysis (meta- and otherwise) of multinational transfer pricing research," *International Journal of Accounting*, 31(1): 39–53.

Borkowski, S.C., M.J. Welsh, and Q. Zhang (2001), "An analysis of statistical power in behavioral accounting research," *Behavioral Research in Accounting*, 13: 63–84.

Brewer, J.K. (1972), "On the power of statistical tests in the American Educational Research Journal," *American Educational Research Journal*, 9(3): 391–401.

Brock, J. (2003), "The 'power' of international business research," *Journal of International Business Studies*, 34(1): 90–99.

Cashen, L.H. and S.W. Geiger (2004), "Statistical power and the testing of null hypotheses: A review of contemporary management research and recommendations for future studies," *Organizational Research Methods*, 7(2): 151–167.

Chase, L.J. and R.B. Chase (1976), "A statistical power analysis of applied psychological research," *Journal of Applied Psychology*, 61(2): 234–237.

Clark-Carter, D. (1997), "The account taken of statistical power in research published in the British Journal of Psychology," *British Journal of Psychology*, 88(1): 71–83.

Cohen, J. (1962), "The statistical power of abnormal-social psychological research: A review," *Journal of Abnormal and Social Psychology*, 65(3): 145–153.

Cohen, J. (1988), Statistical Power for the Behavioral Analysis, 2nd Edition. Hillsdale: Lawrence Erlbaum.

Cohen, J. (1990), "Things I have learned (so far)," *American Psychologist*, 45(12): 1304–1312.

Cohen, J. (1992), "A power primer," *Psychological Bulletin,* 112(1): 155–159.

Ellis, P.D., (2010a) "Effect sizes and the interpretation of research results in international business," *Journal of International Business Studies,* 41(9): 1581–1588.

Ellis, P.D. (2010b), *The Essential Guide to Effect Sizes: An Introduction to Statistical Power, Meta-Analysis and the Interpretation of Research Results,* Cambridge University Press.

Faul, F., E. Erdfelder, A.G. Lang, and A. Buchner (2007), "G*Power 3: A flexible statistical power analysis program for the social, behavioral, and biomedical sciences," *Behavior Research Methods,* 39(2): 175–191.

Faul, F., E., Erdfelder, A., Buchner, and A.G. Lang (2009), "Statistical power analyses using G*Power 3.1: Tests for correlation and regression analyses," *Behavior Research Methods,* 41: 1149–1160.

Fisher, R.A. (1925), *Statistical Methods for Research Workers.* Edinburgh: Oliver and Boyd.

Green, S.B. (1991), "How many subjects does it take to do a regression analysis?" *Multivariate Behavioral Research,* 26(3): 499–510.

Hung, K.H., F. Gu, and C.K. Yim (2007), "A social institutional approach to identifying generation cohorts in China with a comparison with American consumers," *Journal of International Business Studies*, 38(5): 836–853.

Ioannidis, J.P.A. (2005), "Why most published research findings are false," *PLoS Med*, website www.plosmedicine.org/article/info:doi/10.1371/journal.pmed.0020124, 696–701.

Kelley, K. and S.E. Maxwell (2008), "Sample size planning with applications to multiple regression: Power and accuracy for omnibus and targeted effects," in P. Alasuutari, L. Bickman, and J. Brannen (editors), *The Sage Handbook of Social Research Methods*, London: Sage, 166–192.

Kerr, N.L. (1998), "HARKing: Hypothesizing after the results are known," *Personality and Social Psychology Review*, 2(3): 196–217.

Kolata, G.B. (1981), "Drug found to help heart attack survivors," *Science*, 214(13): 774–775.

Kosciulek, J.F. and E.M. Szymanski (1993), "Statistical power analysis of rehabilitation research," *Rehabilitation Counseling Bulletin*, 36(4): 212–219.

Kroll, R.M. and L.J. Chase (1975), "Communication disorders: A power analytic assessment of recent research," *Journal of Communication Disorders*, 8(3): 237–247.

Lindsay, R.M. (1993), "Incorporating statistical power into the test of significance procedure: A methodological and empirical inquiry," *Behavioral Research in Accounting*, 5: 211–236.

Magnusson, P., D.W. Baack, S. Zdravkovic, K.M. Staub, and L.S. Amine (2008), "Meta-analysis of cultural differences: Another slice at the apple," *International Business Review,* 17(5): 520–532.

Mazen, A.M., L.A. Graf, C.E. Kellogg, and M. Hemmasi (1987), "Statistical power in contemporary management research," *Academy of Management Journal,* 30(2): 369–380.

McSwain, D.N. (2004), "Assessment of statistical power in contemporary accounting information systems research," *Journal of Accounting and Finance Research,* 12(7): 100–108.

Mone, M.A., G.C. Mueller, and W. Mauland (1996), "The perceptions and usage of statistical power in applied psychology and management research," *Personnel Psychology,* 49(1): 103–120.

Orme, J.G. and T.D. Combs-Orme (1986), "Statistical power and Type II errors in social work research," *Social Work Research and Abstracts,* 22(3): 3–10.

Reus, T.H. and D. Rottig (2009), "Meta-analyses of international joint venture performance determinants: Evidence for theory, artifacts and the unique context of China," *Management International Review,* 49(5): 607–640.

Rossi J.S. (1990), "Statistical power of psychological research: What have we gained in 20 years?" *Journal of Consulting and Clinical Psychology,* 58(5): 646–656.

Sawyer, A.G. and A.D. Ball (1981), "Statistical power and effect size in marketing research," *Journal of Marketing Research,* 18(3): 275–290.

Singh, J. (2007), "Asymmetry of knowledge spillovers between MNCs and host country firms," *Journal of International Business Studies,* 38(5): 764–786.

Sedlmeier, P. and G. Gigerenzer (1989), "Do studies of statistical power have an effect on the power of studies?" *Psychological Bulletin,* 105(2): 309–316.

Shoham, A. (2003), "Standardization of international strategy and export performance: A meta-analysis," in E. Kaynak (ed.) *Strategic Global Marketing: Issues and Trends*. Haworth Press: 97–120.

Tihanyi, L., D.A. Griffith, and C.J. Russell (2005), "The effect of cultural distance on entry mode choice, international diversification, and MNE performance: A meta-analysis," *Journal of International Business Studies,* 36(3): 270–283.

Zhao, H.X., Y.D. Luo, and T.W. Suh (2004), "Transaction cost determinants and ownership-based entry mode choice: A meta-analytical review," *Journal of International Business Studies,* 35(6): 524–544.

Zumbo, B.D. and A.M. Hubley (1998), "A note on misconceptions concerning prospective and retrospective power," *The Statistician,* 47 (Part2): 385–388.

www.ingramcontent.com/pod-product-compliance
Lightning Source LLC
LaVergne TN
LVHW020048110826
845155LV00029B/686

9781927230572